I0213348

Descendants of Robert Winthrop & Kate Wilson Taylor

1833 - 2000

COPYRIGHT © 2007 BY JOHN WINTHROP

All rights reserved. No part of this publication may be reproduced, distributed, or transmitted in any form or by any means, including photocopying, recording, or other electronic or mechanical methods, without the prior written permission of the publisher, except in the case of brief quotations embodied in certain noncommercial uses permitted by copyright law.

Printed in the United States of America.

ISBN 978-0-9970242-2-7

J Winthrop, Charleston, South Carolina

www.winthropfamily.org

INTRODUCTION

Kate Wilson Taylor, daughter of Moses Taylor, a man of considerable means, married Robert Winthrop on June 23, 1859. Robert Winthrop, born on August 18, 1833, was a Wall Street banker who founded Robert Winthrop & Company in the early 1870's.

It should be remembered that the first seven generations of the Winthrop family – tracing a direct line to the first Governor of Massachusetts – provided a less challenging picture since only one son of each generation produced male issue. All of this history is well documented in The Winthrop Family in America, by Lawrence Shaw Mayo (Massachusetts Historical Society, 1948).

During the last half century, the numbers expanded very rapidly with all members of our tribe able to document their lineage not only to the man who founded Boston, but several other well-known ancestors as well. Many of whom had names that did not begin with "W"!

As the reader surveys the names in this book it is important to remember that each of us has over one thousand ancestors, if we go back eleven generations (counting parents, grandparents, great grandparents, etc.). The final portion of this effort is devoted to putting our family tree into a far broader perspective. For most of us the Genome Experiment (A National Geographic-IBM partnership effort) is worth a glance.

*   *   *

Why take the time to develop and update a family tree? The answer is complicated. With four sons and two grandsons, this effort has been prepared for them – at least in part. The hope, of course, is that some members of the broader family might find it of some interest, despite any errors that might appear.

No doubt there was some selfish interest in tackling this particular genealogical task. I simply wanted to see how the "roadmap" to each expanding family looked and, as the eldest male Winthrop of the eleventh generation in America, I felt a vague responsibility to create the charts.

DEDICATION

To the "Holy Family."

OVERVIEW

A glance into the distant past ...

First Generation:	John Winthrop
Second Generation:	John Winthrop, Jr.
Third Generation:	Wait Still Winthrop
Fourth Generation:	John Winthrop
Fifth Generation:	John Still Winthrop
Sixth Generation:	Francis Bayard Winthrop
Seventh Generation:	Thomas Charles Winthrop
Eighth Generation:	Robert Winthrop

Ninth Generation:	Robert Dudley Winthrop	(no marriage, no children)
	Grenville Lindall Winthrop	(m. Mary Talmadge Trevor)
	Katharine Taylor Winthrop	(m. Hamilton Fish Kean)
	Frederic Bayard Winthrop	(m. Dorothy Amory; Sarah Thayer)
	Albertina Taylor Winthrop	(m. Jan Herman van Roijen)
	Beekman Winthrop	(m. Melza Riggs Wood)

(Read *The Winthrop Family in America* for more details.)

TENTH GENERATION

Grenville Lindall Winthrop and Mary Talmadge Trevor

Emily Lindall Winthrop	m. Corey Lucien Miles
Kate Winthrop	m. Darwin Spurr Morse

Katharine Taylor Winthrop and Hamilton Fish Kean

John Kean	m. Mary Alice Priscilla Barney
Robert Winthrop Kean	m. Elizabeth Stuyvesant Howard

Frederic Bayard Winthrop and Dorothy Amory

Robert Winthrop	m. Theodora Ayer
	m. Margaret Stone
	m. Floreine J. Nelson
Dorothy Winthrop	m. Standish Bradford
Frederic Winthrop	m. Angela Forbes

Frederic Bayard Winthrop and Sarah Barrol Thayer

Nathaniel Winthrop	m. Serita Bartlett
	m. Eleanor R. Beane
John Winthrop	
Katharine Winthrop	m. Quincy Adams Shaw McKean

Albertina Taylor Winthrop and Jan Herman van Roijen

Jan Herman van Roijen	m. Anne Snouck Hurgronje
Robert Dudlen van Roijen	m. Hildegarde Portner Graham

Beekman Winthrop and Melza Riggs Wood

No issue

ELEVENTH GENERATION – MORSE

Kate Winthrop and Darwin Spurr Morse

Thomas Spurr Morse   m. Patricia Birt
Robert Floyd Morse   m. Irene Florence Cleator

ELEVENTH GENERATION – KEAN

John Kean and Mary Alice Priscilla Barney

Mary Alice Raynolds	m. David Robert Wallace Raynolds
John Kean	m. Joan Emily Jessup
	m. Pamela Summers
Stewart Barney Kean	

Robert Winthrop Kean and Elizabeth Stuyvesant Howard

Elizabeth Stuyvesant Hicks	m. Edward Livingston Hicks III
Robert Winthrop Kean, Jr.	m. Luz Maria Silverio
	m. Sandra Johnson
	m. Katherine Tobeason
Hamilton Fish Kean, II	m. Ellen Shaw Garrison
	m. Alice N. Baker
	m. Edie H. Kean
Rose Anthony Kean	m. Edgar George Lansbury
Thomas Howard Kean	m. Deborah Elizabeth Bye
Katharine Winthrop Kean	

ELEVENTH GENERATION – WINTHROP, BRADFORD

Robert Winthrop and Theodora Ayer

Theodora Winthrop	m. Thomas Lee Higginson
	m. Bruce Hooten
Elizabeth Amory Winthrop	m. Francis Ellsworth Baker, Jr.
	m. Herbert Scott Snead
	m. Malcolm Pennington Ripley
	m. Phillip Shatz
Cornelia Beekman Winthrop	m. Edward Shelby Bonnie

Dorothy Winthrop and Standish Bradford

Dorothy Amory Bradford	m. Arthur Wexler
Standish Bradford	m. Brigitte Pullerdt
Katharine Bradford	
Elizabeth Gardner Bradford	m. Gavin Borden

Frederic Winthrop and Angela Forbes

Iris Angela Frederica Winthrop	m. Willard Clark Freeman
Angela Winthrop	m. Charles Willard Getchell
Adam Winthrop	m. Miranda Townsend McCagg
Frederic Winthrop	m. Susan Bailey Shaw
Robert Winthrop	m. Carol Veatch
Grant Forbes Winthrop	m. Hope Harley Brock
Jonathan Winthrop	m. Sydney Cheston

ELEVENTH GENERATION – WINTHROP

Nathaniel T. Winthrop and Serita Bartlett

John Winthrop	m. Deborah Holbrook
	m. Elizabeth Goltra
Matthew B. Winthrop	
Beekman Winthrop	m. Phoebe Jane Wood
Serita Winthrop	m. Robert Martin Barzun
	m. Jonathan Alexander
	m. Thomas McCants

Nathaniel T.Winthrop and Eleanor R. Beane

Nathaniel T. Winthrop	m. Martha Dunn
Katharine Winthrop	m. Peter Hagen
Cornelia Thayer Winthrop	
Stephen van Rensselaer Winthrop	m. Jane Williamson

Katharine Winthrop and Quincy Adams Shaw McKean

John Winthrop McKean	
Thomas McKean	m. Sylvia Wyman
Robert Winthrop McKean	m. Sandra Naomi Kanenaka
Sally Thayer McKean	
David McKean	m. Kathleen Kaye

ELEVENTH GENERATION – VAN ROIJEN

Jan Herman van Roijen and Anne Snouck Hurgronje

Henriette Robertina van Roijen	m. Michiel van Notten
Jan Herman Robert Dudley van Roijen	m. Carolien Helena Wilhelmina Reuchlin
Digna Ann van Roijen	m. Jan derck van Karnebeek
Willem Joris John Winthrop van Roijen	m. Emilie Solange van Nispen

Robert Dudley van Roijen and Hildegarde Portner Graham

Robert Dudley van Roijen	m. Susan Emily Frelinghuysen
Melza Van Roijen	
Peter Portner van Roijen	m. Beatrice Sterling Frelinghuysen
Hildegarde Roberta Valaer van Roijen	m. John Alden Goodrich
Laura Winthrop van Roijen	m. Willem de Vogel
David Montrolse van Roijen	m. Amie Johnson
Christopher Taylor van Roijen	

TWELFTH GENERATION – MORSE

Thomas Spurr Morse and Patricia Morse

Jeffrey Birt Morse m. Carol Gingles
Kate Winthrop Morse m. John D. Erwin
 m. Thomas Landes Horn

Amy Bradford Morse m. Philip Harding (dec.)
Peter Darwin Morse m. Karen Foycik

Robert Floyd Morse and Irene Florence Cleator

No issue

TWELFTH GENERATION – RAYNOLDS

Mary Alice Raynolds and David Wallace Raynolds

Robert Gregory Honshu Raynolds   m. Mary Vera Batholomay
Linda Shikoku Raynolds
Martha Kean Raynolds   m. Samuel Solomon Dashevsky
Laura Teresa Raynolds   m. Alexander Blackmer
David Alan Fernando Raynolds   m. Sharon Elisabeth Bolles

TWELFTH GENERATION – KEAN

John Kean and Joan Emily Jessup

Mary Lita Kean	m. Frederick L. Haack
John Kean, Jr.	m. Abigail M. Murphy
Katharine Jessup Kean	m. David Czarnecki
Susan Livingston Kean	m. Dino G. Cattaneo

TWELFTH GENERATION – HICKS, KEAN, LANSBURY

Elizabeth Stuyvesant Kean and Edward Livingston Hicks, III

Edward Livingston Hicks, IV	m. Kathy Maxwell
Elizabeth Stuyvesant Hicks	m. Peter Wheelwright
Cynthia Montgomery Hicks	m. Peter W. Niles
	m. R. Westbye Cutting
Stephen Winthrop Hicks	m. Elizabeth Hazan

Robert Winthrop Kean, Jr. and Luz Maria Silverio

Robert Winthrop Kean, III	m. Patricia Coxe Patterson
	m. Mallory Gibbs Blimm
Peter Stuyvesant Kean	m. Susan Carow
Alexander Livingston Kean	m. Laurel Jean Hope
	m. Ina Eichhof
Ana Maria Kean	
Nicholas Kean	m. Mary Margaret Kirk Groome
Christopher Kean	

Hamilton Fish Kean and Ellen Shaw Garrison

Leslie Barlow Kean	m. John McKim
	m. Jerry Rosser
Elizabeth Stuyvesant Kean	m. Philip Douglas
Lloyd Garrison Kean	
Lewis Morris Kean	m. Anne Squire

Rose Anthony Kean and Edgar George Lansbury

James Edgar Lansbury	m. Susan Snorf
Michael Bruce Lansbury	m. Janet Johnson
David Anthony Lansbury	m. Alexandra Sheedy
George Winthrop Lansbury	m. Emily Bickford
Brian McIldowie Lansbury	m. Tasha Cornell
Katharine Rose Lansbury	

Thomas Howard Kean and Deborah Elizabeth Bye

Thomas Howard Kean, Jr. m. Rhonda Lee Norton

Reed Stuyvesant Kean

Alexandra Dickinson Kean m. Benjamin Strong

Katherine Winthrop Kean

TWELFTH GENERATION – HIGGINSON, BONNIE

Theodora Winthrop and Thomas Lee Higginson
Thomas Lee Higginson, Jr.	m. Feroline Perkins Burrage
Elizabeth Higginson	m. Larry Alan Rideman
Robert Winthrop Higginson	m. Judy Ann Jones

Cornelia Beekman Winthrop and Edward Shelby Bonnie
Shelby Winthrop Bonnie	m. Carol Navone
Robert Farrell Bonnie	m. Cynthia Polk
	m. Julie Gomena

TWELFTH GENERATION –
BRADFORD, WEXLER, BORDEN

Dorothy Amory Bradford and Arthur Wexler

Dorothy Amory Wexler   m. Luke Ali Sadrian

Jacob Winthrop Wexler   m. Sari Yoshioka

Standish Bradford and Brigitte Pullendert

Tatyana Amory Bradford   m. J. Timothy Ouhrabka

Amanda Dorothy Bradford

Standish Bradford, III

Elizabeth Gardner Bradford and Gavin Borden

Sarah Gardner Borden   m. John Wareck

Gavin Hamilton Borden

Frederic Amory Nalle Borden

TWELFTH GENERATION –
FREEMAN, GETCHELL, WINTHROP

Iris Angela Frederica Winthrop and Willard Clark Freeman
Michael Winthrop Freeman   m. Jessie Milne

Angela Winthrop and Charles Willard Getchell
Katharine Chisolm Getchell   m. Robert Clark
Emily Erskine Getchell   m. Gabriel Grenot-Portoundo
Sarah Fields Getchell

Adam Winthrop and Miranda Townsend McCagg
Angela Frederica Winthrop
Miranda Rosemary Winthrop

Frederic Winthrop and Susan Bailey Shaw
Rebecca Winthrop   m. Ron Monahan
Frederic Winthrop, III   m. Alice Helen MacInnes
Laura Winthrop
Robert Shaw Winthrop

Robert Winthrop and Carol Veatch
Margaret Katherine Winthrop

Grant Forbes Winthrop and Hope Hartley Brock
Elizabeth Hartley Winthrop   m. Adin Ryan Murray
Fernanda Wood Winthrop
Charlotte Brock Winthrop

Jonathan Winthrop and Sydney Cheston
Georgina Cheston Winthrop
Augusta Amory Winthrop

TWELFTH GENERATION – WINTHROP, BARZUN, HAGEN

John Winthrop and Deborah Holbrook

John Winthrop, Jr.   m. Louisa Daley
Henry Grenville Winthrop
Bayard Winthrop

John Winthrop and Elizabeth Goltra

Edward Field Winthrop

Matthew Bartlett Winthrop

No issue

Beekman Winthrop and Phoebe Jane Wood

Dudley Winthrop   m. Jennifer Louise Snee

Serita Winthrop and Roger Martin Barzun

Mariana Lowell Barzun   m. Jon Mensch
Matthew Winthrop Barzun   m. Brooke Brown
Lucretia Mott Barzun   m. Robert Donnelly
Charles Lowell Barzun

Nathaniel T. Winthrop and Martha Dunn

Elias Dunn Winthrop
Emma O'Meara Winthrop
Daniel Winthrop

Katharine Thayer Winthrop and Peter Hagan

Taylor Bonnet Hagan
Robert Christopher Powell Hagan

Stephen van Rensselaer Winthrop and Jane Williamson

Casey Winthrop
Hannah Winthrop

TWELFTH GENERATION –
MCKEAN

John Winthrop McKean
No issue

Thomas McKean and Sylvia Wyman
Adam Shaw McKean
Matthew Thornton McKean
Benjamin Pierce McKean

Robert Winthrop McKean and Sandra Naomi Kananaka
Robert Winthrop McKean, Jr.
Sarah Naomi McKean
John Pratt McKean

Sally Thayer McKean
No issue

David McKean and Kathleen Kaye
Shaw Forbes McKean
Christian Kallin McKean
Kay Thayer McKean

TWELFTH GENERATION –
VAN NOTTEN, VAN ROIJEN, VAN KARNEBEEK

Henriette Albertina van Roijen and Michiel van Notten

Anne Marina van Notten	m. Jan Petit
Henriette Digna Albertina Winthrop van Notten	m. Reindert C.F.E. Houben
Isabelle van Notten	m. David Rosenberg
Ariane van Notten	m. Harold Fentener van Vlissingen

Jan Herman Robert Dudley van Roijen and Carolien Helena Wilhalmina Reuchlin

Jan Herman van Roijen	m. Sophie Charlotte Egbertine van der Kuip
Anne van Roijen	
Theodora Helena Wilhelmina van Roijen	m. Frank van den Merkenhof

Digna Anne van Roijen and Jan Derek van Karnebeek

Jan Derek van Karnebeek	m. Jacqueline Thijsen
Emile Thelma van Karnebeek	m. Jeroen Pit
Clara Digna van Karnebeek	

Willem Joris John Winthrop van Roijen and Emile Solange van Nispen

Joris Willem Peter van Roijen
Robert Dudley van Roijen

TWELFTH GENERATION –
VAN ROIJEN, GOODRICH

Robert Dudley van Roijen and Susan Emily Frelinghuysen
> Victoria Frelinghuysen van Roijen
> Valaer Montrose van Roijen

Peter Portner van Roijen and Beatrice Sterling Frelinghuysen
> Theodora Albertina van Roijen
> Linden Frelinghuysen van Roijen
> Peter Matthew van Roijen

Hildegarde Roberta Valaer van Roijen and John Alden Goodrich
> Lauren Valaer Goodrich
> John Alden Goodrich, Jr.
> Winthrop Pullen Graham Goodrich

David Montrose van Roijen and Amie Johnson
> David Berend van Roijen
> Melza Riding van Roijen

THIRTEENTH GENERATION –
MORSE, ERWIN, HARDING

Jeffrey Birt Morse and Carol Gingles
Joshua Elias Morse
Jason Cooper Morse

Kate Winthrop Morse Horn and John David Erwin
Cathryn Birt Erwin
Elliot Winthrop Erwin

Amy Bradford Morse and Philip Harding (dec.)
Chloe Callan Morse Harding
Lila Morse Harding

Peter Darwin Morse and Karen Foycik
Lucas Tyler Morse
James Thomas Morse
Gabrielle Morse

THIRTEENTH GENERATION –
RAYNOLDS, BLACKMER

Robert Gregory Honshu Raynolds and Mary Vera Batholomay
William Fremont Peter Raynolds
Robert Kean Lackman Raynolds

Martha Kean Raynolds and Samuel Solomon Dashevsky
Marguerite Nularvik Dashevsky
Daniel Sithylemenkat Dashevsky
Sophia Kanuti Dashevsky

Laura Teresa Raynolds and Alexander Blackmer
Courtney Kean Blackmer Raynolds
Lisa Dexter Blackmer Raynolds

David Alan Fernando Raynolds and Sharon Elisabeth Bolles
Jasper Forest Bolles Raynolds
Kyrianna Rose Raynolds Bolles

THIRTEENTH GENERATION –
HAACK, KEAN, CZARNECKI, CATTANEO

Mary Lita Kean and Frederick L. Haack
Alexandra Kean Haack
Benjamin Kean Haack
Christina Kean Haack

John Kean, Jr. and Abigail M. Murphy
John Kean, III
Margaret Emily Kean
Elizabeth Murphy Kean
Henry Livingston Kean

Katharine Jessup Kean and David Czarnecki
Sarah Elizabeth Czarnecki
Johanna Errickson Czarnecki
Isabelle Williams Czarnecki

Susan Livingston Kean and Dino G. Cattaneo
Nicholas Everett Cattaneo
Charlotte Kean Cattaneo

THIRTEENTH GENERATION – HICKS, WHEELWRIGHT, NILES

Edward Livingston Hicks, IV and Kathy Maxwell

Sarah Livingston Hicks
Jessica Maxwell Hicks

Elizabeth Stuyvesant Hicks and Peter Wheelwright

Elizabeth Hicks Wheelwright
Josephine Kean Wheelwright
Peter Matthiessen Wheelwright

Cynthia Montgomery Hicks and Peter W. Niles

Orion Mansfield Niles
Eliza Joy Niles
Julia Kean Niles

Stephen Winthrop Hicks and Elizabeth Hazan

Benjamin Bayard Hicks
Katharine Taylor Hicks
Lucien E. Hicks

THIRTEENTH GENERATION – KEAN, MCKIM, DOUGLAS

Robert Winthrop Kean, Jr. and Patricia Coxe Patterson
    Robert Winthrop Kean, IV
    Philip Edward Patterson Kean
    Christina Dear Kean

Peter Stuyvesant Kean and Susan Carow
    Jesse Carow Kean
    Hallie Elizabeth Kean   m. Joshua Council

Alexander Livingston Kean and Laurel Jean Hope
    Adam Kean
    Jediah Kean

Nicholas Kean and Mary Margaret Kirk Groome
    Schuyler Livingston Kirk Kean
    Nicholas Miximillian Winthrop Kean

Leslie Barlow Kean and John McKim
    Paul Alexander McKim

Elizabeth Stuyvesant Kean and Philip Douglas
    Elizabeth Shaw Douglas
    Samuel Garrison Douglas
    Henry Hamilton Douglas

Lewis Morris Kean and Anne Squire
    Nicholas Squire Kean
    Simon Garrison Kean

THIRTEENTH GENERATION – LANSBURY

James Edgar Lansbury and Susan Snorf
    Charles Edgar Lansbury
    Robert Buffett Lansbury
    Galen Kean Lansbury
    William James Lansbury
    Thomas Howard Lansbury

Michael Bruce Lansbury and Janet Johnson
    Charlotte Rose Lansbury
    Madeline Virginia Lansbury
    Benjamin Lansbury

David Anthony Lansbury and Alexandra Sheedy
    Rebecca Elizabeth Lansbury

George Winthrop Lansbury and Emily Bickford
    Elizabeth Laura Lansbury
    Natalie Rose Taber Lansbury

Brian McIldowie Lansbury and Tasha Cornell
    Quinn Lansbury
    Macklin Kean

THIRTEENTH GENERATION – KEAN

Thomas Howard Kean, Jr. and Rhonda Lee Norton
    Elizabeth Winthrop Kean
    Meredith Lee Kean

Alexdra Dickinson Kean and Benjamin Strong
    Katharine Kean Strong
    Thomas Brewster Strong

THIRTEENTH GENERATION – HIGGINSON, RIDEMAN

Thomas L. Higginson and Feroline Perkins Burrage
Theodora Winthrop Higginson
Henry Lee Higginson

Elizabeth Higginson and Larry Alan Rideman
Miranda Claire Rideman

Robert Winthrop Higginson and Judy Ann Jones
Jeremy Joseph Higginson
Aurelia Anne Higginson

THIRTEENTH GENERATION – BONNIE

Shelby Winthrop Bonnie and Carol Navone
Mason Winthrop Bonnie
Henry Sevier Bonnie
Virginia Ayer Bonnie

Robert Farrell Bonnie and Cynthia Polk
Lily Bonnie

Robert Farrell Bonnie and Julie Gomena
No issue

THIRTEENTH GENERATION – SADRIAN, WEXLER

Dorothy Amory Wexler and Luke Ali Sadrian
Arthur Ian Sadrian

Jacob Winthrop Wexler and Sari Yoshioka
Yuji Art Yoshioka Wexler
Hanami Amy Yoshioka Wexler

THIRTEENTH GENERATION – OUHRABKA

Tatyana Amory Bradford and Jan Timothy Ouhrabka

    Jan Chase Ouhrabka

    Thatcher Bradford Ouhrabka

    Alexis Amory Ouhrabka

THIRTEENTH GENERATION – WARECK

Sarah Gardner Borden and John Wareck
Anya Gardner Wareck
Stella Rose Wareck

THIRTEENTH GENERATION – FREEMAN

Michael Winthrop Freeman and Jessie Adams Milne

No issue

THIRTEENTH GENERATION – CLARK, GRENOT

Katharine Chisholm Getchell and Robert Clark

    Max Clark

Emily Erskine Getchell and Gabriel Grenot-Portuondo

    Cassius Grenot

    Ulysses Grenot

THIRTEENTH GENERATION – CLARK, GRENOT

Rebecca Winthrop and Ron Monahan
Riley Winthrop Monahan
Fiona Winthrop Monahan

Frederic Winthrop, III and Alice Helen McInnes
No issue

THIRTEENTH GENERATION – MURRAY

<u>Elizabeth Hartley Winthrop and Adin Ryan Murray</u>
No issue

THIRTEENTH GENERATION – WINTHROP

Robert Winthrop > Nathaniel Winthrop > John Winthrop > John Winthrop, Jr.

John Winthrop, Jr. and Louisa Daley

John Bradford Winthrop
Robert Daley Winthrop

THIRTEENTH GENERATION –
MENSCH, BARZUN

Mariana Lowell Barzun & Jon Mensch

Elizabeth Mensch

Claire Mensch

Matthew Winthrop Barzun and Brooke Brown

Eleanor Barzun

Jacques Barzun

Charles Winthrop Barzun

THIRTEENTH GENERATION –
PETIT, HOUBEN, ROSENBERT, VAN VLISSINGEN

Anne Marina van Notten and Jan Petit
Milan Max Petit

Isabelle Oriana Petit

Ruben Robert Petit

Henriette Digna Albertina Winthrop van Notten
and Reindert Carl Frans Edward Houben
Francesca Digna Albertina Houben

Dante Houben

Isabelle van Notten and David Rosenbert
Sarah Juliet Rosenberg van Notten

Ariane van Notten and Harold Fentener van Vlissingen
Frederick Hayek Fentener van Vlissingen

Daniel Nelson Fentener van Vlissingen

Livia Fentener van Vlissingen

THIRTEENTH GENERATION –
VAN ROIJEN, VAN MERKENHOF

Jan Herman Van Roijen and Sophie Charlotte Egbertine van der Kuip
Jan Herman Marnix van Roijen

Theodora Helena Wilhelmina van Roijen and Frank van den Merkenhof
No issue

THIRTEENTH GENERATION – VAN KARNEBEEK

Jan Derek van Karnebeek and Jacqueline Thijsen
Herman Adriaan van Karnebeek

Emilie Thelma van Karnebeek and Jeroen Pit
Isabelle Anne Karnebeek

FOURTEENTH GENERATION – COUNCIL

Hallie Elizabeth Kean and Joshua Council
    Jacob Council

FOURTEENTH GENERATION – KEAN

Adam Kean and Katrina Patterson
Cassidy Kean

Mary Jane Kean

Adam Kean and Carolina Monza
Giulia Monza Kean

Ian Monza Kean

A footnote ...

The Big Picture – Genetic History

In order to put our ancestry into proper perspective, I decided to participate in the Genographic Project – a research partnership of IBM and National Geographic.

My assumption was that many of us in the broader family had roughly the same origins and so I sent the appropriate material for scientific research in the early part of 2006.

Some of the results may be of passing interest ...

1) Our genetic markers, defining our ancestral history, go back roughly 60,000 years.

2) The gene trail, left by all non-African men, goes over a very long route from the heart of East Africa to Western Europe (see map).

3) About seventy percent of all men in Southern England belong to the same gene group ("Haplo Group R1B").

4) All of us carry DNA that is passed on by our mothers and fathers. Eye color, height, disease resistance and other qualities can be traced this way, but the Y chromosome is passed from father to son only.

5) Without a mutation, a marker can be traced for thousands of years, but each shift can identify the beginning of a new branch of the family tree of the human race.

6) More information is being gathered by additional volunteers. In time a more complete picture will result. Now we can be certain of the broad outlines of our journey. We all came from Africa about 50,000 years ago at which time there were approximately 10,000 Homo sapiens! While the first evidence of humankind moving out of Africa may have started 50-60,000 years ago, we can also find evidence of "anatomically modern humans" evolving in Africa 200,000 years ago.

7) It can be concluded that most of the journey of our distant ancestors was motivated by availability of game and climate change.

8) About 40,000 years ago our first joint ancestor had probably located in Iran of southern Central Asia. This was called the "Eurasian Clan" in the history books. Most of us native to the Northern Hemisphere share this heritage.

9) Then, about 35,000 years ago our marker suggests movement to Kazakhstan, Uzbekistan and Southern Siberia.

10) About 30,000 years ago, with an estimated population of Homo sapiens around 100,000, the tribes headed west – toward the European sub-continent. As our ancestors inched their way into Europe, artistic skills, scientific skills and general intelligence is said to have blossomed.

We are the final step in that long journey. Stay tuned for further elaboration as more genome evidence becomes available, but always remember the monkeys are our cousins.

NOTE: Our path, as depicted on the map, goes from
M168 to M89 to M9 to M45 to M207 to M173 to M343.

J.W.

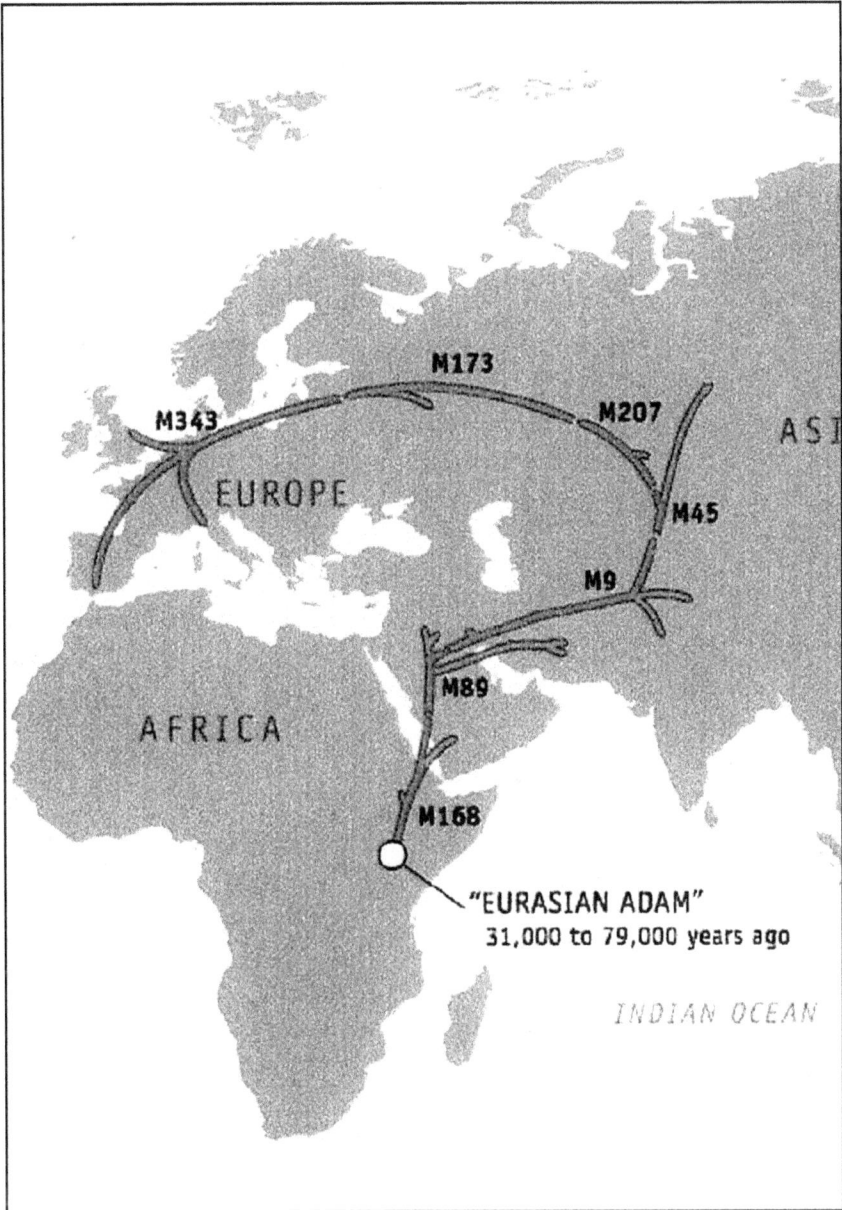

"EURASIAN ADAM"
31,000 to 79,000 years ago

www.ingramcontent.com/pod-product-compliance
Lightning Source LLC
Chambersburg PA
CBHW070830100426
42813CB00003B/560

* 9 7 8 0 9 9 7 0 2 4 2 2 7 *